David Hendra Music

EASY CELLO CHRISTMAS CAROLS

Book One

Twenty traditional Christmas carols and hymns
for easy violoncello

by
David Hendra

EASY CELLO CHRISTMAS CAROLS - Book One
Twenty traditional Christmas carols and hymns for easy violoncello

Carol and hymn lyrics and melodies are in the public domain.
Notation, bowing and fingering for 'cello by David Hendra.

ISBN: 9798338125304

Contents

Brief History Of The Violoncello

The violoncello, or *'cello*, is a remarkable instrument known for its deep, rich tones. Let's take a quick journey through time and discover its origins and evolution:

The Early Days

The 'cello's ancestors date back to 16th century Italy, where instruments like the viola da gamba began to make their mark. The 'cello as we know it emerged in the early 17th century. Master luthiers in Cremona, Italy, designed the 'cello to be a more a versatile and dynamic bass instrument, as required by the new compositions of the time.

The Cremonese Masters

Early makers, such as the Amati family, Andrea Guarneri, and Antonio Stradivari, made important contributions to 'cello development. Their instruments exhibited both rich, powerful sound and exquisite craftsmanship. The standards they set are still revered to this day.

The Golden Age

In the 18th century, composers such as Bach, Haydn, and Boccherini elevated the 'cello from a background to a solo instrument, in what is often considered the golden age of 'cello music. Bach's *Six Suites for Unaccompanied Cello* remain some of the most beloved pieces in the cello repertoire, challenging and enchanting 'cellists and audiences alike for centuries.

The Cello Evolves

Over the years, the 'cello was modified to enhance its sound and playability. For example, the endpin (or spike) was more widely added in the 19th century to allowing 'cellists to play a fuller sound more easily. During the Romantic era, composers like Dvorák and Elgar wrote concertos that showcased both the emotional range and the technical capabilities of the 'cello.

The Cello Today

The 'cello is a cornerstone of orchestras, chamber music, and solo performances, loved for its expression and adaptability. Today's composers and 'cellists continue to explore its possibilities, blending traditional and new techniques to create new sounds and innovative performances.

The violoncello has come a long way from the workshops of Italian luthiers in the 1500s to today's concert halls. As you find your own journey with your 'cello, you're joining a centuries-old tradition of artistry and passion. Enjoy!

Looking After Your Cello

Handle with Care
Always hold your ‘cello by the neck or the sides. Don’t touch the ‘cello's body more than you need to; keep it clean from skin oils, dirt and dust.

Tuning
Use an app or electronic tuner for accuracy. Turn the pegs gently to avoid snapping the strings. If unsure, get help and advice from a teacher or a professional.

Cleaning
After playing, wipe down your ‘cello and strings with a soft, dry cloth to remove rosin dust and fingerprints. If possible, use separate cloths for the body and the strings.

Environment
Cellos don't like extreme conditions. Try to keep yours in stable humidity (45-70%) and temperature (around 70°F or 21°C). Don’t leave it near a heat source or in a car.

Storage
Store your ‘cello in a case with the latches or zip closed to protect it from dust and damage. Don't leave it standing on its endpin (spike) or on its back unprotected.

Bow Care
Loosen the bow hair after use. Don’t touch the hair; skin oils can damage it.

String Replacement
Keep your ‘cello sounding at its best by changing the strings at least once a year, or sooner if they begin to sound dull.

Health Checks
If possible, have a luthier check your ‘cello annually, to catch any potential issues early, such as open seams or cracks.

Minor Repairs
Perhaps learn how to reposition your bridge if it shifts, but leave any other significant repairs to the experts!

Rosin:
Rosin your bow sparingly. Residue can collect and harm the finish of your ‘cello; too much rosin can make the sound harsh, too.

How To Use Your FREE mp3 Tracks

There are 40 free mp3 audio tracks to accompany this book.

20 DEMO tracks
The DEMO mp3 files contain the melody, played through ***once.*** You will hear beats at the start, so you know when to join in:
If the melody **starts on beat one**, you will hear **two full bars of beats** at the start.
If the melody **starts on a different beat**, you will hear **one full bar and one part bar.**

Use the DEMO tracks during your practice, to check you are playing the correct notes and that you are in tune..

20 BACKING tracks
The BACKING mp3 files contain professionally arranged accompaniments that you can use both during practice and for performing. Each track has a brief musical introduction, followed by an accompaniment to your sheet music played through ***twice.***

Downloading
To download a track, follow the link on the sheet music page and select it from the list. Depending on your device and browser, you may be able to click and play the mp3 file straight from the page. Alternatively, *right*-click to download it for future use.

Copyright
You may use the linked mp3 files for your personal practice, and to accompany your public performance if you wish. However, please do not copy or distribute them elsewhere. Thank you for respecting copyright.

1. Angels From The Realms Of Glory

Tune: IRIS

(French carol melody)

Arranged by David Hendra

Download your FREE tracks for this carol:

davidhendramusic.com/cello-carols1

(see the ***How To Use Your FREE mp3 Tracks*** page)

Angels from the realms of glory,
Wing your flight o'er all the earth;
Ye who sang creation's story,
Now proclaim Messiah's birth:
Come and worship,
Come and worship,
Worship Christ, the newborn King!

Shepherds, in the fields abiding,
Watching o'er your flocks by night,
God with man is now residing,
Yonder shines the infant Light;
Come and worship,
Come and worship,
Worship Christ, the newborn King!

Sages, leave your contemplations,
Brighter visions beam afar;
Seek the great desire of nations,
Ye have seen His natal star;
Come and worship,
Come and worship,
Worship Christ, the newborn King!

Saints before the altar bending,
Watching long in hope and fear,
Suddenly the Lord, descending,
In His temple shall appear:
Come and worship,
Come and worship,
Worship Christ, the newborn King!

James Montgomery 1771-1854

2. As With Gladness Men Of Old

Tune: DIX

(from a chorale by Conrad Kocher 1786-1772)

Arranged by David Hendra

Download your FREE tracks for this carol:

davidhendramusic.com/cello-carols1

(see the ***How To Use Your FREE mp3 Tracks*** page)

As with gladness men of old
Did the guiding star behold
As with joy they hailed its light
Leading onward, beaming bright
So, most gracious God, may we
Evermore be led to Thee

As with joyful steps they sped
To that lowly manger bed
There to bend the knee before
Thee whom heaven and earth adore
So may we with willing feet
Ever seek Thy mercy-seat

As they offered gifts most rare
At that manger rude and bare
So may we with holy joy
Pure, and free from sin's alloy
All our costliest treasures bring
Christ, to Thee, our heavenly King

Holy Jesus, every day
Keep us in the narrow way
And, when earthly things are past
Bring our ransomed souls at last
Where they need no star to guide
Where no clouds Thy glory hide.

In the heavenly country bright
Need they no created light
Thou its light, its joy, its crown
Thou its sun, which goes not down.
There forever may we sing
Hallelujahs to our King

William Chatterton Dix 1837-1898

3. Brightest And Best

Tune: EPIPHANY HYMN

(Joseph Francis Thrupp 1827-1867)

Arranged by David Hendra

Download your FREE tracks for this carol:

davidhendramusic.com/cello-carols1

(see the ***How To Use Your FREE mp3 Tracks*** page)

Brightest and best of the sons of the morning,
Dawn on our darkness and lend us Thine aid;
Star of the East, the horizon adorning,
Guide where our infant Redeemer is laid.

Cold on His cradle the dewdrops are shining;
Low lies His head with the beasts of the stall;
Angels adore Him in slumber reclining,
Maker and Monarch and Saviour of all!

Say, shall we yield Him, in costly devotion,
Odours of Edom and offerings divine?
Gems of the mountain and pearls of the ocean,
Myrrh from the forest, or gold from the mine?

Vainly we offer each ample oblation,
Vainly with gifts would His favour secure;
Richer by far is the heart's adoration,
Dearer to God are the prayers of the poor.

Brightest and best of the sons of the morning,
Dawn on our darkness and lend us Thine aid;
Star of the East, the horizon adorning,
Guide where our infant Redeemer is laid.

Reginald Heber 1783-1826

4. Christians, Awake!

Tune: YORKSHIRE

(John Wainwright 1723-1768)

Arranged by David Hendra

Download your FREE tracks for this carol:

davidhendramusic.com/cello-carols1

(see the ***How To Use Your FREE mp3 Tracks*** page)

Christians, awake, salute the happy morn,
Whereon the Saviour of the world was born;
Rise to adore the mystery of love,
Which hosts of angels chanted from above;
With them the joyful tidings were begun
Of God incarnate and the Virgin's son.

Then to the watchful shepherds it was told,
Who heard th'angelic herald's voice: "Behold,
I bring good tidings of a Saviour's birth
To you and all the nations on the earth:
This day hath God fulfilled his promised word,
This day is born a Saviour, Christ the Lord."

He spake, and straightway the celestial choir
In hymns of joy, unknown before, conspire;
The praises of redeeming love they sang,
And heav'n's whole orb with alleluias rang;
God's highest glory was their anthem still,
Peace on the earth, and unto men good will.

To Bethl'hem straight the happy shepherds ran,
To see the wonder God had wrought for man;
And found, with Joseph and the blessed maid,
Her son, the Saviour, in a manger laid;
Amazed, the wondrous story they proclaim,
The earliest heralds of the Saviour's name.

Oh, may we keep and ponder in our mind
God's wondrous love in saving lost mankind!
Trace we the babe, who hath retrieved our loss,
From his poor manger to his bitter cross.
Tread in his steps, assisted by his grace,
Till our imperfect state God doth replace.

Then may we hope, th'angelic throngs among,
To sing, redeemed, a glad triumphal song;
He that was born upon this joyful day
Around us all his glory shall display;
Saved by his love, incessant we shall sing
Eternal praise to heav'n's almighty King.

John Byrom 1692-1763

5. Deck The Halls

Tune: NOS GALAN
(Welsh dance tune)

Arranged by David Hendra

Download your FREE tracks for this carol:

davidhendramusic.com/cello-carols1

(see the ***How To Use Your FREE mp3 Tracks*** page)

Deck the halls with boughs of holly,
Fa, la, la, la, la, la, la, la, la!
'Tis the season to be jolly,
Fa, la, la, la, la, la, la, la, la!
Don we now our gay apparel,
Fa, la, la, la, la, la, la, la, la!
Troll the ancient Christmas carol,
Fa, la, la, la, la, la, la, la, la!

See the blazing yule before us,
Fa, la, la, la, la, la, la, la, la!
Strike the harp and join the chorus.
Fa, la, la, la, la, la, la, la, la!
Follow me in merry measure,
Fa, la, la, la, la, la, la, la, la!
While I tell of Christmas treasure,
Fa, la, la, la, la, la, la, la, la!

Fast away the old year passes,
Fa, la, la, la, la, la, la, la, la!
Hail the new, ye lads and lasses!
Fa, la, la, la, la, la, la, la, la!
Sing we joyous all together,
Fa, la, la, la, la, la, la, la, la!
Heedless of the wind and weather,
Fa, la, la, la, la, la, la, la, la!

Thomas Oliphant 1799–1873

6. God Rest Ye Merry, Gentlemen

Tune: GOD REST YE MERRY
(Traditional English melody)

Arranged by David Hendra

Download your FREE tracks for this carol:

davidhendramusic.com/cello-carols1

(see the ***How To Use Your FREE mp3 Tracks*** page)

God rest ye merry, gentlemen, let nothing you dismay
Remember, Christ, our Saviour was born on Christmas day
To save us all from Satan's power when we were gone astray

O tidings of comfort and joy, comfort and joy
O tidings of comfort and joy

In Bethlehem, in Israel this blessed Babe was born
And laid within a manger upon this blessed morn
The which His Mother Mary did nothing take in scorn

O tidings of comfort and joy...

From God our Heavenly Father a blessed Angel came
And unto certain Shepherds brought tidings of the same
How that in Bethlehem was born the Son of God by Name

O tidings of comfort and joy...

"Fear not then", said the Angel, "Let nothing you affright
This day is born a Saviour of a pure Virgin bright
To free all those who trust in Him from Satan's power and might"

O tidings of comfort and joy...

The shepherds at those tidings rejoiced much in mind
And left their flocks a-feeding in tempest, storm and wind
And went to Bethlehem straightway the Son of God to find

O tidings of comfort and joy...

And when they came to Bethlehem where our dear Saviour lay
They found Him in a manger where oxen feed on hay
His Mother Mary kneeling down unto the Lord did pray

O tidings of comfort and joy...

Now to the Lord sing praises all you within this place
And with true love and brotherhood each other now embrace
This holy tide of Christmas all other doth deface

O tidings of comfort and joy...

Traditional English carol

7. Good King Wenceslas

Tune: TEMPUS ADEST FLORIDUM

(from Piae Cantiones, 1582)

Arranged by David Hendra

Download your FREE tracks for this carol:

davidhendramusic.com/cello-carols1

(see the ***How To Use Your FREE mp3 Tracks*** page)

Good King Wenceslas looked out
On the feast of Stephen
When the snow lay round about
Deep and crisp and even
Brightly shone the moon that night
Though the frost was cruel
When a poor man came in sight
Gath'ring winter fuel

"Hither, page, and stand by me
If thou know'st it, telling
Yonder peasant, who is he?
Where and what his dwelling?"
"Sire, he lives a good league hence
Underneath the mountain
Right against the forest fence
By Saint Agnes' fountain."

"Bring me flesh and bring me wine
Bring me pine logs hither
Thou and I will see him dine
When we bear him thither."
Page and monarch forth they went
Forth they went together
Through the rude wind's wild lament
And the bitter weather

"Sire, the night is darker now
And the wind blows stronger
Fails my heart, I know not how,
I can go no longer."
"Mark my footsteps, my good page
Tread thou in them boldly
Thou shalt find the winter's rage
Freeze thy blood less coldly."

In his master's steps he trod
Where the snow lay dinted
Heat was in the very sod
Which the Saint had printed
Therefore, Christian men, be sure
Wealth or rank possessing
Ye who now will bless the poor
Shall yourselves find blessing

John Mason Neale 1818-1866

8. Hark, The Herald Angels Sing

Tune: MENDELSSOHN

(Felix Mendelssohn-Bartholdy 1809-1915)

Arranged by David Hendra

Download your FREE tracks for this carol:

davidhendramusic.com/cello-carols1

(see the ***How To Use Your FREE mp3 Tracks*** page)

Hark the herald angels sing
"Glory to the newborn King!
Peace on earth and mercy mild
God and sinners reconciled"
Joyful, all ye nations rise
Join the triumph of the skies
With the angelic host proclaim:
"Christ is born in Bethlehem"
Hark! The herald angels sing
"Glory to the newborn King!"

Christ by highest heav'n adored
Christ the everlasting Lord!
Late in time behold Him come
Offspring of a Virgin's womb
Veiled in flesh the Godhead see
Hail the incarnate Deity
Pleased as man with man to dwell
Jesus, our Emmanuel
Hark! The herald angels sing
"Glory to the newborn King!"

Hail the heav'n-born Prince of Peace!
Hail the Son of Righteousness!
Light and life to all He brings
Ris'n with healing in His wings
Mild He lays His glory by
Born that man no more may die
Born to raise the sons of earth
Born to give them second birth
Hark! The herald angels sing
"Glory to the newborn King!"

Charles Wesley 1707-1788

9. I Cannot Tell

Tune: LONDONDERRY AIR

(Irish traditional melody)

Arranged by David Hendra

Download your FREE tracks for this carol:

davidhendramusic.com/cello-carols1

(see the ***How To Use Your FREE mp3 Tracks*** page)

I cannot tell why He, whom angels worship,
Should set His love upon the sons of men,
Or why, as Shepherd, He should seek the wand'rers,
To bring them back, they know not how or when.
But this I know, that He was born of Mary,
When Bethl'hem's manger was His only home,
And that He lived at Nazareth and laboured,
And so the Saviour, Saviour of the world, is come.

I cannot tell how silently He suffered,
As with His peace He graced this place of tears,
Or how His heart upon the Cross was broken,
The crown of pain to three and thirty years.
But this I know, He heals the broken-hearted,
And stays our sin, and calms our lurking fear,
And lifts the burden from the heavy laden,
For yet the Saviour, Saviour of the world, is here.

I cannot tell how He will win the nations,
How He will claim His earthly heritage,
How satisfy the needs and aspirations
Of east and west, of sinner and of sage.
But this I know, all flesh shall see His glory,
And He shall reap the harvest He has sown,
And some glad day His sun shall shine in splendour
When He the Saviour, Saviour of the world, is known.

I cannot tell how all the lands shall worship,
When, at His bidding, every storm is stilled,
Or who can say how great the jubilation
When all the hearts of men with love are filled.
But this I know, the skies will thrill with rapture,
And myriad, myriad human voices sing,
And earth to heaven, and heaven to earth, will answer:
At last the Saviour, Saviour of the world, is King.

William Young Fullerton 1857-1932

10. In The Bleak Midwinter

Tune: CRANHAM
(Gustav Holst 1874-1934)

Arranged by David Hendra

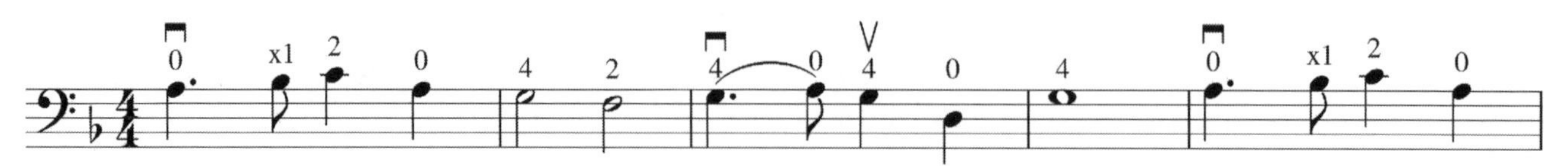

Download your FREE tracks for this carol:

davidhendramusic.com/cello-carols1

(see the ***How To Use Your FREE mp3 Tracks*** page)

In the bleak mid-winter
Frosty wind made moan;
Earth stood hard as iron,
Water like a stone;
Snow had fallen, snow on snow,
Snow on snow,
In the bleak mid-winter
Long ago.

Our God, heaven cannot hold Him
Nor earth sustain,
Heaven and earth shall flee away
When He comes to reign:
In the bleak mid-winter
A stable-place sufficed
The Lord God Almighty —
Jesus Christ.

Angels and Archangels
May have gathered there,
Cherubim and seraphim
Thronged the air;
But only His Mother
In her maiden bliss
Worshipped the Beloved
With a kiss.

What can I give Him,
Poor as I am? —
If I were a Shepherd
I would bring a lamb;
If I were a Wise Man
I would do my part, —
Yet what I can I give Him, —
Give my heart.

Christina Georgina Rosetti 1830-1894

11. It Came Upon The Midnight Clear

Tune: NOEL

(English traditional melody)

Download your FREE tracks for this carol:

davidhendramusic.com/cello-carols1

(see the ***How To Use Your FREE mp3 Tracks*** page)

It came upon the midnight clear,
That glorious song of old,
From angels bending near the earth
To touch their harps of gold:
"Peace on the earth, good will to men,
From heaven's all-gracious King."
The world in solemn stillness lay,
To hear the angels sing.

Still through the cloven skies they come
With peaceful wings unfurled,
And still their heavenly music floats
O'er all the weary world;
Above its sad and lowly plains,
They bend on hovering wing,
And ever o'er its Babel sounds
The blessed angels sing.

And ye, beneath life's crushing load,
Whose forms are bending low,
Who toil along the climbing way
With painful steps and slow,
Look now! for glad and golden hours
Come swiftly on the wing.
O rest beside the weary road,
And hear the angels sing!

For lo! the days are hastening on,
By prophet seen of old,
When with the ever-circling years
Shall come the time foretold
When peace shall over all the earth
Its ancient splendors fling,
And the whole world send back the song
Which now the angels sing.

Edward Hamilton Sears 1810-1876

12. Love Came Down At Christmas

Tune: HERMITAGE

(Reginald Owen Morris 1886-1948)

Arranged by David Hendra

Download your FREE tracks for this carol:

davidhendramusic.com/cello-carols1

(see the ***How To Use Your FREE mp3 Tracks*** page)

Love came down at Christmas,
Love all lovely, Love divine;
Love was born at Christmas,
Star and angels gave the sign.

Worship we the Godhead,
Love incarnate, Love divine;
Worship we our Jesus:
But wherewith for sacred sign?

Love shall be our token,
Love be yours and love be mine,
Love to God and all men,
Love for plea and gift and sign.

Christina Georgina Rosetti 1830-1894

13. O Come, All Ye Faithful

Tune: ADESTE FIDELES
(John Francis Wade 1711-1786)

Arranged by David Hendra

Download your FREE tracks for this carol:

davidhendramusic.com/cello-carols1

(see the ***How To Use Your FREE mp3 Tracks*** page)

O come, all ye faithful, joyful and triumphant!
O come ye, O come ye to Bethlehem;
Come and behold him
Born the King of Angels:
O come, let us adore Him,
O come, let us adore Him,
O come, let us adore Him,
Christ the Lord.

God of God, light of light,
Lo, he abhors not the Virgin's womb;
Very God, begotten, not created:
O come, let us adore Him,
O come, let us adore Him,
O come, let us adore Him,
Christ the Lord.

Sing, choirs of angels, sing in exultation,
Sing, all ye citizens of Heaven above!
Glory to God, glory in the highest:
O come, let us adore Him,
O come, let us adore Him,
O come, let us adore Him,
Christ the Lord.

Yea, Lord, we greet thee, born this happy morning;
Jesus, to thee be glory given!
Word of the Father, now in flesh appearing!
O come, let us adore Him,
O come, let us adore Him,
O come, let us adore Him,
Christ the Lord.

Translated from 18th century Latin by Frederick Oakley 1802-1880

14. O Holy Night!

Tune: CANTIQUE DE NOEL

(Adolph Charles Adam 1803-1856)

Arranged by David Hendra

Download your FREE tracks for this carol:

davidhendramusic.com/cello-carols1

(see the ***How To Use Your FREE mp3 Tracks*** page)

O holy night, the stars are brightly shining,
It is the night of the dear Saviour's birth;
Long lay the world in sin and error pining,
'Till he appeared and the soul felt its worth.
A thrill of hope the weary world rejoices,
For yonder breaks a new and glorious morn;

Fall on your knees, Oh hear the angel voices!
O night divine! O night when Christ was born.
O night, O holy night, O night divine.

Led by the light of Faith serenely beaming;
With glowing hearts by his cradle we stand:
So, led by light of a star sweetly gleaming,
Here come the wise men from Orient land,
The King of Kings lay thus in lowly manger,
In all our trials born to be our friend;

He knows our need, To our weakness no stranger!
Behold your King! Before Him lowly bend!
Behold your King! your King! before him bend!

Truly He taught us to love one another;
His law is Love and His gospel is Peace;
Chains shall he break, for the slave is our brother,
And in his name all oppression shall cease,
Sweet hymns of joy in grateful Chorus raise we;
Let all within us praise his Holy name!

Christ is the Lord, then ever! ever praise we!
His pow'r and glory, evermore proclaim!
His pow'r and glory, evermore proclaim!

Placide Cappeau 1808-1877

15. Once In Royal David's City

Tune: IRBY

(Henry John Gauntlett 1805-1876)

Arranged by David Hendra

Download your FREE tracks for this carol:

davidhendramusic.com/cello-carols1

(see the ***How To Use Your FREE mp3 Tracks*** page)

Once in royal David's city,
Stood a lowly cattle shed,
Where a mother laid her baby
In a manger for His bed:
Mary was that mother mild,
Jesus Christ her little child.

He came down to earth from heaven,
Who is God and Lord of all,
And His shelter was a stable,
And His cradle was a stall;
With the poor and meek and lowly,
Lived on earth our Saviour holy.

And through all His wondrous childhood,
He would honour and obey,
Love and watch the lowly mother,
In whose gentle arms He lay.
Christian children all should be,
Mild, obedient, good as He.

For He is our childhood's pattern,
Day by day like us He grew,
He was little, weak, and helpless,
Tears and smiles like us He knew,
And He feeleth for our sadness,
And He shareth in our gladness.

And our eyes at last shall see Him,
Through His own redeeming love;
For that child so dear and gentle,
Is our Lord in heaven above,
And He leads His children on,
To the place where He is gone.

Not in that poor lowly stable,
With the oxen standing by,
We shall see Him, but in heaven,
Set at God's right hand on high;
When like stars his children crowned,
All in white shall be around.

Cecil Frances Alexander 1818-1895

16. Silent Night

Tune: STILLE NACHT
(Franz Gruber 1787-1863)

Arranged by David Hendra

Download your FREE tracks for this carol:

davidhendramusic.com/cello-carols1

(see the ***How To Use Your FREE mp3 Tracks*** page)

Silent night, holy night!
All is calm, all is bright.
Round yon Virgin, Mother and Child.
Holy infant so tender and mild,
Sleep in heavenly peace,
Sleep in heavenly peace

Silent night, holy night!
Shepherds quake at the sight.
Glories stream from heaven afar
Heavenly hosts sing Alleluia,
Christ the Saviour is born!
Christ the Saviour is born

Silent night, holy night!
Son of God love's pure light.
Radiant beams from Thy holy face
With the dawn of redeeming grace,
Jesus Lord, at Thy birth
Jesus Lord, at Thy birth

Joseph Mohr 1792-1848
(translated by Stopford Augustus Brooke)

17. The First Nowell

Tune: THE FIRST NOWELL
(English traditional carol)

Arranged by David Hendra

Download your FREE tracks for this carol:

davidhendramusic.com/cello-carols1

(see the ***How To Use Your FREE mp3 Tracks*** page)

The first nowell the angel did say
Was to certain poor shepherds in fields as they lay;
In fields where they lay keeping their sheep
On a cold winter's night that was so deep.

Nowell, nowell, nowell, nowell,
Born is the King of Israel.

They lookèd up and saw a star
Shining in the east beyond them far;
And to the earth it gave great light,
And so it continued both day and night.

Nowell, nowell...

And by the light of that same star
Three wise men came from country far;
To seek for a king was their intent,
And to follow the star wherever it went.

Nowell, nowell...

This star drew nigh to the north-west:
O'er Bethlehem it took its rest;
And there it did both stop and stay,
Right over the place where Jesus lay.

Nowell, nowell...

Then entered in those wise men three,
Full reverently upon their knee,
And offered there, in his presence,
Their gold and myrrh and frankincense.

Nowell, nowell...

Then let us all with one accord
Sing praises to our heavenly Lord
Who hath made heaven and earth of nought,
And with his blood mankind hath bought.

Nowell, nowell...

Anonymous (17th century)

18. Thou Didst Leave Thy Throne

Tune: MARGARET

(Timothy Richard Matthews 1826-1910)

Arranged by David Hendra

Download your FREE tracks for this carol:

davidhendramusic.com/cello-carols1

(see the ***How To Use Your FREE mp3 Tracks*** page)

Thou didst leave Thy throne and Thy kingly crown,
When Thou camest to earth for me;
But in Bethlehem's home was there found no room
For Thy holy nativity.
O come to my heart, Lord Jesus,
There is room in my heart for Thee.

Heaven's arches rang when the angels sang,
Proclaiming Thy royal degree;
But of lowly birth didst Thou come to earth,
And in great humility.
O come to my heart, Lord Jesus,
There is room in my heart for Thee.

The foxes found rest, and the birds their nest
In the shade of the forest tree;
But Thy couch was the sod, O Thou Son of God,
In the deserts of Galilee.
O come to my heart, Lord Jesus,
There is room in my heart for Thee.

Thou camest, O Lord, with the living word
That should set Thy people free;
But with mocking scorn, and with crown of thorn,
They bore Thee to Calvary.
O come to my heart, Lord Jesus,
There is room in my heart for Thee.

When the heavens shall ring, and the angels sing,
At Thy coming to victory,
Let Thy voice call me home, saying "Yet there is room,
There is room at My side for thee."
My heart shall rejoice, Lord Jesus,
When Thou comest and callest for me.

Emily Elizabeth Steele Elliott 1836-1897

19. We Three Kings

Tune: KINGS OF ORIENT

(John Henry Hopkins 1820-1891)

Arranged by David Hendra

Download your FREE tracks for this carol:

davidhendramusic.com/cello-carols1

(see the ***How To Use Your FREE mp3 Tracks*** page)

We three kings of Orient are;
Bearing gifts we traverse afar,
Field and fountain, moor and mountain,
Following yonder star.

O star of wonder, star of light,
Star with royal beauty bright,
Westward leading, still proceeding,
Guide us to thy perfect light.

Born a King on Bethlehem's plain,
Gold I bring to crown him again,
King forever, ceasing never,
Over us all to reign.

O star of wonder...

Frankincense to offer have I;
Incense owns a Deity nigh;
Prayer and praising, voices raising,
Worshiping God on high.

O star of wonder...

Myrrh is mine; its bitter perfume
Breathes a life of gathering gloom;
Sorrowing, sighing, bleeding, dying,
Sealed in the stone-cold tomb.

O star of wonder...

Glorious now behold him arise;
King and God and sacrifice:
Alleluia, Alleluia,
Sounds through the earth and skies.

O star of wonder...

John Henry Hopkins 1820-1891

20. While Shepherds Watched

Tune: WINCHESTER OLD

(George Kirbye 1565-1634)

Arranged by David Hendra

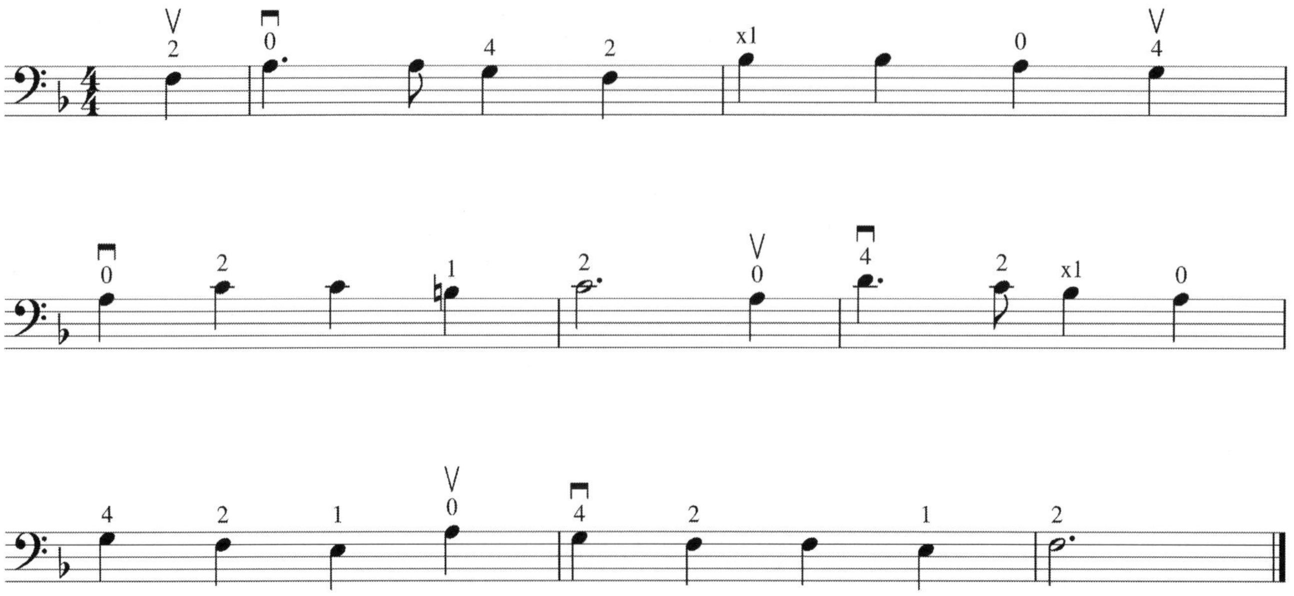

Download your FREE tracks for this carol:

davidhendramusic.com/cello-carols1

(see the ***How To Use Your FREE mp3 Tracks*** page)

While shepherds watched their flocks by night,
All seated on the ground,
The angel of the Lord came down,
And glory shone around.

"Fear not," said he, for mighty dread
Had seized their troubled mind;
"Glad tidings of great joy I bring
To you and all mankind.

"To you, in David's town, this day
Is born of David's line
A Saviour, who is Christ the Lord;
And this shall be the sign:

"The heavenly Babe you there shall find
To human view displayed,
All meanly wrapped in swathing bands,
And in a manger laid."

Thus spake the seraph, and forthwith
Appeared a shining throng
Of angels praising God, who thus
Addressed their joyful song:

"All glory be to God on high
And on earth be peace;
Goodwill henceforth from heaven to men
Begin and never cease."

Nahum Tate 1652-1715

A personal note from David...

Thank you for choosing this book from David Hendra Music..

Unlike the big publishers, with their army of specialist writers, compilers, arrangers, designers, proof-readers and distributors, I'm an independent publisher on Amazon and I do *everything* myself!

So... if you find a mistake or something you think I could do better, please email: *david@easypianoteacher.com.* I reply to all emails, and your suggestions will be considered for this and future books from DHM.

IMPORTANT: If you enjoy this book, PLEASE leave a positive review on Amazon. Your five-star feedback *really* helps to get my work seen by other learners. I would appreciate your support!

I wish you every success on your musical learning journey. Get in touch with your ideas, or if I can be of service to you.

David

PS: turn to the next page for your ***FREE BONUSES!***

FREE BONUSES!

Would you like to learn piano, too?

BONUS 1:

get your **FREE** eBook and find out about learning piano ***without*** a teacher!

Download your copy at

easypianoteacher.com/16reasons

BONUS 2:

Try the **COMPLETELY FREE** piano tutorials at

easypianoteacher.com

Made in the USA
Las Vegas, NV
07 December 2024